Your Book Is Now

How to Become a Self-Published Author

Second Edition

DEMARQUIS BATTLE

ISBN: 9781986515818

DEDICATION

I continue to write and develop resources to be an encouragement to the next generation. This book is for anyone who desires to put their dreams on paper, see their vision flourish, and witness their purpose come alive.

CONTENTS

INTRODUCTION

Everyone has a story. Few people dare to write it. In this original and insightful book, I share my experience of going through the self-publishing process. Follow the blueprint as I take you through eight critical steps to self-publishing, and as I share with you how to earn additional income as a self-publishing company. In this second edition, I will also share some new graphic design tools, marketing strategies, and updates to some of the pricing models and publishing platforms. Don't wait for the perfect circumstance to write the book you've always dreamed of. Decide today that your book is now.

1 START NOW

One day, after speaking to a group of high school students, my mentor made a comment that ignited something inside of me. He said, "I can see you writing a book." I never considered doing this before, but my goal of impacting the next generation caught hold of his encouraging words. I immediately began to dream big. I saw myself using the content of my books (yes, I envisioned more than one), to share a message of hope. I believed I could empower high school students and young adults around the world.

A few days after my speaking engagement, and after receiving encouragement from my mentor to write a book, I started to do some self-reflection. I began to envision walking in my purpose as an educator at a higher level and thought to myself, "I'm tired of working the common nine to five." Don't get me wrong, I still have a day job, but I was tired of allowing it to rule me. I never wanted to do the usual thing or be placed in a box. In my heart, I knew there was something more significant.

Have you ever felt this way? Tired of the mundane and ready for a change? Feeling marginal or insignificant is frustrating, but at the same time, having this feeling, when finessed correctly, it can create a sense of hope and excitement for possibilities on the horizon. This is what moves you to the next level of action. The frustrations with average and the desire for greatness, it pushes you. It drives you. It calls out to you. It motivates you to seek out your purpose and to walk in it ultimately. I realized my calling was to share my story as an author and impact the next generation as an entrepreneur and speaker.

I knew what I desired precisely. My dream of becoming an author and functioning as an entrepreneur was just a fingertip away. Just like the lion in the childhood classic, the Wizard of Oz, all I needed was a little courage. In fact, most individuals who desire to do something great, battle the same thing—which is the fear of failure.

What I eventually learned was fear is meant to keep you stagnate. Caught in a rut. Indecisive and uncertain of yourself. When you're in this position, you never fall too far into the pit of failure that your dream dies. At the same time, you never really move forward enough in your business venture to see your idea grow legs and walk. This is an unfortunate place for an optimistic dreamer. You can dream about writing your book, but at some point, you have to move from dreaming to doing. You must take hold of courage, move forward, jump out, and start now.

It is also said if you ever want to succeed, you may have to be willing to do something crazy, bold, and challenging. Authors don't wait for convenience. They start writing immediately when a story pops in their head. Entrepreneurs don't wait for someone to consider their product, and they don't allow barriers to stop them from achieving their goals. Both overcome various challenges, despite the odds stacked against them.

When the support is nonexistent from family and friends, keep going. When the finances are low, and you lack resources, keep moving. Push yourself. Just like a skydiver gazing through the doorway of a plane, the only way to overcome the fear is just to jump out. The remarkable thing about jumping out is you get past the fear of failure quickly.

You realize the fact you are deciding to do this constitutes your first victory. Most of your peers and colleagues who aspire to be authors and/or entrepreneurs are waiting for a warm and fuzzy feeling to pursue their dream. Don't be the person who waits for everything to be perfect, because it will never be the case. How many kids dream of getting on the biggest and fastest roller coaster at an amusement park but let fear inhibit their experience and they never get on? Don't let the fear of failure extinguish your desire to start your own business or write a book. Just jump and start now. When I say jump out, I don't mean aimlessly hope for the best. All principles still apply. Hard work, integrity, and passion, just to name a few, should be clearly visible in your character. There are no short cuts to success. You reap what you sow, so start sowing seeds of faithfulness, dedication, drive, and determination and see what you harvest. If you want to be great, and you want to accomplish extraordinary things, dream big, jump out, and start your journey as an author and entrepreneur now.

2 START WRITING

When I got home after that speaking engagement, I started writing. I pulled out my laptop, sat down, and I let the words take shape. I thought about the passion I had for youth and my desire to see them be successful. So as I clicked on the keys, I verbally recited each line and paragraph. I did this by pulling from my experiences. I wrote until I literally couldn't write anymore. After you dream big and jump out to become a self-published author, the next step is to begin your story. Just start writing.

I didn't worry about how it sounded, at least not in the beginning stage. I just let ideas roll like a movie and recorded what I saw. Many of you have a blueprint or outline for a book you want to write. The key is setting some time aside to do it. For me, I took my lunch breaks, late nights, and any moment I could find to write. This kept the ideas in my mind fresh. I was sort of like a basketball player who has scored a flurry of baskets. The player is now considered "hot"; therefore, the coach often draws up plays for that player so he can continue to score. The moral of the story is to get "hot" as an author. Don't stop writing when you're on a scoring streak. Let it rain.

I was so passionate about the subject that I rarely

encountered writer's block. The concept, the setup, the transitions, they all just flowed. This is the way it should be when you are writing about something you care about. Maybe you want to share your life story. Perhaps you've always wanted to write a cookbook with cherished recipes that have been handed down through generations of your family. A fictional sci-fi novel might be your cup of tea. Whatever the story, gain enough courage to start writing.

There are a couple different ways you can go about writing your story. For me, I used the standard word processor on my laptop. Others find it convenient to write in a journal. Some will even record themselves electronically and then transcribe the recording. You have to determine what is best for you. Whatever the method, be sure you have the right way of keeping track of your progress and content. If you are using a computer, be sure to back up your manuscript in multiple places (i.e., flash drive, hard drive, cloud space).

Another thing I found helpful for developing my manuscript(s) was to jot down any spur of the moment idea I had. Sometimes inspiration will come to you while you're eating your lunch or when you're tucked into bed, getting ready to fall asleep. I recommend keeping a pad of paper and a pen or some other way of recording your ideas, conveniently close by. You never know if that one idea will be the major breakthrough needed for your story.

Another exciting element I found when writing my first book was you're always adding to the manuscript. I'd watch television, and something that was said inspired me to add new content to the book. Sometimes driving down the highway and seeing a billboard may spark a new idea in my heart. Utilize your surroundings. Receive from people and places that are often overlooked. You may find some hidden treasure in those moments that will make your book even more valuable.

Another area of importance for authors is, taking periodic breaks from your manuscript. Your brain must rest, so your thoughts are coherent. Your break can be hours, days, or a week. I wouldn't go any longer than that, because you don't want to stifle your productivity. At the same time, don't be afraid to walk away for a moment to re-energize. It will make for a better manuscript.

Once you finish the first draft of your book, you will move on to the editing process. This is the area that will take up most of your time. The first mistake many indie authors make is relying heavily on their word processor's "spell check" feature as the sole means of editing. As you may be aware, this will address some of your grammatical errors, but it won't catch everything. You have to become diligent as a self-published author and entrepreneur to get it right.

This may mean you hire someone to do the editing for you. There are professional services you can utilize that are searchable online. I would also encourage you not to ignore co-workers and acquaintances for editing services. They may have access to people who can help you in this department. Your friends are certainly not professionals, but they can at least be honest with you and share their opinion of your manuscript. They may even catch some minor errors by merely being the second pair of eyes.

On my first project, I worked with a friend who was an educator. She had extensive knowledge of reviewing papers and manuscripts. If you feel comfortable using someone like this, make sure you develop some type of formal agreement. It is essential to do your due diligence to ensure you are not shortchanging yourself. It may be cost-effective to use a familiar face, but when it comes to editing, you can ill afford to be cheap. A poorly written manuscript can become a turnoff. For nothing other than peace of mind, you may want to consider professional editors. This can be a bit intimidating, but will probably yield better results. At the end of the day, you want to feel confident you've introduced a manuscript to the public that has been professionally vetted.

As a rule of thumb, you should complete as many rounds of editing as you feel needed to produce a polished product.

The standard for most authors is a minimum of three rounds. The author does the first of these edits, including grammar, content, formatting, and more. A few select individuals whose opinions you trust may do the second round of edits. They can review the manuscript for many of the errors missed in the first round and can be used as a filter to catch the residual debris you didn't notice. Lastly, a professional editor can comb through your manuscript to ensure the content, structure, and flow all match. These individuals are often paid at a higher level because of their expertise and accuracy rate.

Now that your editing is completed, you are one step closer to publishing your very own book, but where do you go from here? How do you get this excellent new book into the hands of readers? It is going to take some effort for this next step to be accomplished. In the next chapter, you will learn how to research the process of self-publishing your book with a POD (print-on-demand) service.

3 START BUILDING

Congratulations! Your manuscript is complete. You've made it quite far. Moving forward, you will need to determine how to transform that newly formed manuscript into an actual book (print and electronic) and how you plan to dominate the shelves of retailers nationwide. The first step in getting your book published is to start doing research on the internet. There is so much information available, so you have to be specific with your internet searches. Some keywords I used to help find the right process to publish my manuscript were:

- Self-publishing company
- Print on demand
- Writing my own book
- Publishing my own book
- Publishing secrets
- Becoming an author

Needless to say, I found a ton of results. Eventually, I came across someone who was a successful self-published author who provided resources for others to become the same.

From this information, I learned of several options for me to not only self-publish my very first book but to develop a self-publishing company.

The first option I found was **Createspace (now known as KDP "Kindle Direct Publishing").** This company is owned by Amazon. It gives authors the ability to self-publish print and electronic books. It is considered a print-on-demand service, which means there is no overstocked inventory. Traditionally, authors are on the hook for ordering an initial amount of books from their publisher. If they don't sell all of the books ordered, they are left with hundreds of copies sitting in their garage or basement collecting dust. Print-on-demand allows for the author's book to be printed and sent off when the book is purchased, whether it's one book or one hundred. This helps the author immensely because he or she doesn't need to worry about inventory and unsold books. When you combine the print-on-demand system and that the economic powerhouse, Amazon backs it, you can have a very lucrative business as a self-published author entrepreneur. You are also exposed to the success of Amazon's selling structure when utilizing their online platform. You literally have an international reach that puts your book in the face of consumers worldwide.

To my surprise, KDP was easy to navigate. It walks you through the self-publishing process step-by-step to ensure nothing is missed. The first step is to set up your project. This includes defining your book title, listing the author(s) name, and identifying the publisher. Later in this book, I will highlight the importance of developing a self-publishing company and the freedom it brings to you as an author and an entrepreneur. As you continue moving through the set-up wizard, you will begin filling in the details section of your book. At this point, you can provide recognition of the editors and designers who partnered with you and add the remaining pieces required for most copyright sections. From here you will need to determine the type of ISBN

(International Standard Book Number) you want to use for your book. An ISBN allows your writing to be identified. Usually, a separate ISBN is needed for different variations of your book (i.e., print, electronic, multiple editions). Some systems allow you to publish without one, but it is always recommended for identification and tracking purposes.

For $125 you can obtain an ISBN from Bowker, the only official U.S. ISBN agency. They also have packages of ten and one hundred ISBNs if you plan on publishing several books. This is an excellent way to go if you are writing a series or you desire to get the most bang for your buck.

You can select the free ISBN option that works directly through KDP. This is a cost-effective way to start out as a self-published author, especially if this is your first book. The last option by KDP has actually been eliminated. You can no longer choose a custom ISBN that gave you credit as the publisher with your own publishing signature. I decided on that option in the past because it was cost-effective at only $10, and it had a more professional feel. If you plan to publish your book through another publishing company at a later date, you will need to purchase a new ISBN.

After you have completed the title section and you've selected your ISBN preference, you move on to the next step, which is uploading your manuscript into the system. Kindle Direct Publishing accepts manuscripts in Microsoft Word and pdf formats. The system will give you the necessary guidelines for your document, as well as offer the option of black and white or color interior, and the choice of white or cream paper. KDP will provide you with templates you can use for your manuscript with preloaded text to give you a great idea of what your script should look like. If you are on a budget, KDP also has a la cart features you can purchase that will assist you with the interior of your book. Pricing depends on the amount of assistance you desire. This is helpful if you are looking for a particular look for your text or if you want a specific theme and feel.

If their templates aren't what you're looking for, there are other options. You can find book templates online for an affordable price. One source that has a ton of variety in this area is **bookdesigntemplates.com** by Joel Friedlander of **thebookdesigner.com**. This site has several categorized templates for both print and ebook. The prices vary, but the cheapest template you can find is approximately $59.00, which gives you a single book license. In this license, you will receive the following features:

- Option to use for print and eBook.
- Template compatible with Word, Pages, and InDesign for PC or Mac.
- Innovative 2Way Design for easy eBook creation.
- Includes complete step-by-step instructions.
- Access to their US tech support staff.

In addition to the single book license, you also have a multiple book license that you can use for all of your books. The cost of this license is $119.00. Lastly, you can purchase a commercial use license, which will allow you to become a publishing house and format books for others as a business. The cost of this license is $249.00. Each license comes as a zip folder with the template and the fonts included. I have had experience with using templates from this source and have had pretty good success with it. You can also search for other templates online, many of which are free. You may find a different option that better suits your needs.

Once you have uploaded your manuscript, KDP will prompt their online proofer, that will catch any formatting errors in your document. This is great because you can identify errors on the spot and make changes before you commit to submitting your manuscript for final approval. The system also makes sure your text is not bleeding into the specified guidelines for your manuscript. If upon review, you have determined your document is ready to go, you can save the paper and move on to the next step in the project, which is to upload your book cover. Due to the complex nature of this step and all of the different options, we will highlight it separately in the next chapter.

19

4 START DESIGNING

Just as important as the manuscript itself, the book cover is the key to the success of your book. When consumers are walking down the aisles in Barnes & Noble or searching Amazon online, they are often swayed to stop and look at books that have intriguing covers. Therefore, it is essential that you, as the author, invest wisely in the design of your book cover. As I published my first book, I decided to go with a local designer I knew personally. There are some benefits to this approach. They are as follows:

- **Cost-effective** – working with a local graphic artist will provide low to minimal cost. It's perfectly fine to use the contacts and resources you have, especially if you are on a budget.
- **Speed** – Typically, working with a local graphic artist ensures you obtain your book cover quicker than if you use an online service.
- **Comfort level** – You have the ultimate say of what your book cover looks like when working with a local designer. Depending on whom you work with on the corporate side, whether it is a major publishing company or someone else, your opinion

on the cover may not mean as much. There is a certain amount of comfort working with someone you know.

Now that I have highlighted the positives of working with a local graphic artist, let's take some time to address the negatives you may encounter:

- **Time** – A local graphic artist can be timely, but they can also be late. You want to make sure you have something drawn up contractually that will ensure you sensibly get your book cover.
- **Professionalism** – Local graphic artists have specialty areas just like any other professional. Their main area of design may not be book covers, it may be flyers or social media graphics. You want to make sure what is presented to you represents your vision.

In the end, it will be up to you as the author and publisher to determine which route you want to take. These are not the only options, though. You can decide to design your book cover yourself.

Self-publishing is more than writing a book and selling it. It also includes making decisions about the creative direction of your book. Although it may be difficult, you can design your own book cover with the right tools. One way you can do this is by using graphic design software known as **Adobe Photoshop**. By using this premier graphic design software, you have the potential to produce an excellent book cover. It may take some time for you to get the hang of the features thoroughly, but it can be done. I won't be ignorant and suggest designing a cover is simple as pie. Individuals go to school and dedicate years to this craft, but, in my own experience, I was able to pick things up quickly.

The cost of this software with its new "Adobe creative cloud" varies. At the time of this edition, I pay $20.00 a month to use its system with a monthly "push" update that keeps the software current. KDP will also give you guidelines and requirements for the book cover you are designing. Once you have completed your book cover, you can upload it into the system and eventually do an online proof review. Again, this is a great tool because you can see any detected issues your upload may have and you can make changes immediately.

I recommend submitting a sample of your cover to some of your peers. When doing this, you are not looking for a "yes" answer. You are looking for constructive feedback. As previously stated, your cover is one of the most critical things in the whole self-publishing process. It will cost you more money in the long run if you have to change your book cover later, than getting it done right in the beginning. There are other avenues you can pursue to obtain a dynamic cover for your book. One of those ways is to utilize online services that will create your book cover for you. A company that is highly regarded in the graphic design industry is **99 Designs**. This company has an extensive portfolio of amazing services rendered from web site development, logo creation, and, most importantly, book cover designs.

What makes this service so unique is that you can construct a designing contest where several graphic design artists will create a version of your requested book cover. First, you provide the information for your book cover (title, author name, description, bio, photo, etc.). Then, you allow the professionals to take the creative freedom needed to produce a masterpiece. Within a week you will receive several covers you can pick and choose from. This puts more options in front of you and gives you the power to determine the best fit.

This particular company has different tiers that make up their designing service. The higher the pricing tier, the more dynamic the product. This pricing structure allows for an affordable product but doesn't water down the quality for more serious customers. The pricing breakdown at the time of this edition is as follows:

Bronze Package (good) - $299

- Creative design on a budget
- Approximate 30 designs

Silver Package (better) - $499

- Best value for your money
- Approximate 60 designs

Gold Package (great) - $799

- Expert designers work on your cover
- Approximate 90 designs and an account manager

Platinum Package (best/excellent)

- The very best handpicked designers
- 60 premium designs
- Account manager

This is an excellent example of how a self-published author can make their money work for them. You can still obtain a quality product/service without breaking your budget. As you grow as a self-published author and company, you can decide when it is appropriate to spend more money on cover designs.

Another online option for cover designs is **bookdesigners.com** (different from thebookdesinger.com as previously mentioned for interior templates). They appear to be a bit more expensive with prices ranging from $750-$5,500. They have a similar pricing tier strategy as 99 Designs, but the main difference is this company has a broader range in both pricing and offerings. At the very least, this provides an additional option for you to get your book cover done.

An additional online source to get your book cover completed is with the widely popular **Fiverr**. This company offers tons of different services all for the low price of $5.00 and up. Fiverr has what they call "gigs" and add-ons you can select that range from additional renderings, advanced graphics, or faster delivery of your purchased service. In your case, you may be able to purchase a relatively cheap book cover design for close to nothing. The drawback with this is it may be harder to get what you want because of the nature of the site and the fact it's inexpensive. Generally, you get what you pay for.

If the previously mentioned options don't' seem to work for you, there is still the option of working directly with KDP. There are two choices one can choose when working with KDP on your cover design. They include the custom cover option, which will provide you with a professional-looking cover that captures your vision. The cost is approximately $399. The second option is the custom cover premier. Selecting this option will afford you a professional design team that will develop a compelling book cover showcasing your story's unique elements. The cost of this service is $599. You may not have the necessary funding to go with these options, but don't panic, a new option has exploded on the scene over the last year or two. It's called **Canva**.

This new online design software allows individuals to design presentations, social media graphics, and more with thousands of beautiful layouts. I first got hip to this new site when looking for a platform to create social media graphics *(we will discuss more on this in our marketing section)*. Once I was able to navigate the system and learn more about what it could do, I found that it had awesome templates for designing ebook covers. This was a game-changer. For free, I could design covers for my books that didn't have a cheap feel, and look of being a novice. It actually came off as professional and very clean. At my fingertips, was the ability to control the creative direction of my manuscript and book cover. As a new author and entrepreneur, you can't ask for anything better. Of course, some premium features come at a cost, but in comparison, those charges are minuscule compared to significant publishing and graphic design companies.

Whichever option you decide to go with, make a commitment to yourself that you will be as honest as possible when assessing the quality and creative direction of your cover. There is no need to rush. In fact, you want to take your time with this part of the self-publishing process as the book cover weighs heavily in your success or failure. Once you complete the book cover and upload it, you can move forward with the next step in the self-publishing process. Creating a business that will serve as your book publisher and provide you with the opportunity for an additional revenue stream.

5 START YOUR BUSINESS

Once you have completed your book, you are ready to move forward with developing the structure of your self-publishing company. This is the entrepreneur side of being an author. You want to have a business that will serve as the publisher for every book you write, both print and electronic.

Your self-publishing company will also present speaking opportunities. Authors are known to bring in additional income through this type of business structure. When you publish a book, you are considered an expert on the topic you wrote about. People will be interested to hear you speak in-depth on your subject.

As a self-publishing company, you can earn additional income through speaking engagements and as a self-publishing consultant. Writing and publishing a book can be intimidating, and your personal experiences could help someone else overcome their fears in doing it.

Instead of publishing my book through the traditional route, I determined it was to my benefit to self-publish. I enjoyed the idea of being in control of every phase in the publishing process. It was the scratch I needed to satisfy my entrepreneurial itch. You may feel the same way. So let's break down how to set up your self-publishing company.

The first thing you need to do is determine the type of business structure you want to go with. In most states, the standard business types for a self-publishing company would be a sole proprietorship, corporation, and a limited liability company. Each has its own benefits and challenges. Before I highlight each structure, I want to put out a disclaimer that what I am sharing is not legal advice. It is always essential to seek legal counsel before making any final business decisions. What is presented is my personal experience in starting a self-publishing company.

A **sole proprietorship** is the purest business form under which one can operate a business. The sole proprietorship is not a legal entity. It merely refers to a person who owns the company and is personally responsible for its debts. This might be a good idea if you were operating a speaking business only. But if you plan on writing and selling books, it may make more sense for you to choose a different business structure.

It does have the benefit of accessibility, and its process is not as complicated when completing the paperwork. A sole proprietorship is inexpensive in comparison to the other structures but has more risk involved as well. You assume the debt accumulated because you and the business are considered one and the same. In most states, this is filed with the clerk's office in the county in which you reside.

A **corporation** (sometimes referred to as a **C corporation**) is an independent legal entity owned by shareholders. This means the corporation itself, not the shareholders that own it, is held legally liable for the action sand debts the business incurs. This business structure is often assigned to larger companies and is the most difficult of the three to establish. Again, for what you may be looking for in regards to the flexibility of business for both publishing and speaking, this may not be the appropriate choice for incorporation. Developing corporations tend to be a bit expensive, as well. Paperwork is generally submitted to the state office that houses the licenses and regulations department.

The business structure I selected when forming my self-publishing company was a **limited liability company**. A limited liability company is a hybrid type of legal structure that provides the limited liability features of a corporation and the tax efficiencies and operational flexibility of a partnership. This structure made the most sense for me because it was affordable. The paperwork submission was reasonably straightforward, and it gave me the flexibility to conduct business in several different ways. Incorporation is done in the same fashion as a corporation, which is, with your state office in the licenses and regulations department (this could be titled differently depending on your state).

Now that you have your business structure set up, you need to obtain a federal **Employer Identification Number**. An Employer Identification Number **(EIN)** is also known as a Federal Tax Identification Number and is used to identify a business entity. Generally, businesses need an EIN. You can apply for an EIN in various ways, including online. This is a free service offered by the Internal Revenue Service, and you can get your EIN immediately. You must check with your state to see if you need a state number or charter. For sole proprietorships, you may be able to utilize your social security number. The reason it is crucial to get an EIN is so you can open up a business checking account. This will provide a bank or credit union to have your royalty payments sent to. This will keep your personal and business income separate.

After you have done this, you will be virtually ready to conduct business as an author and entrepreneur with your self-publishing company. As we all know, it will take more for you to be successful as an author and entrepreneur. In the next chapter, we discuss the importance of marketing your book and your business.

6 START MARKETING

You're almost to the point you can start selling books. To do this effectively, you will need to build up some momentum. The best way to do this is through marketing. When I wrote my first book, I had no idea how to market it. I faced many challenges the first go around, but through it, I have become much more prepared to sell my future titles. Although there are many areas of marketing that need to be explored, I would like to highlight the importance of marketing with social media and the web.

It is essential to get connected with various social media platforms to develop a strong web presence. Facebook, Twitter, and Instagram are not only the most recognizable social media platforms, but each of them provides some unique opportunities.

Facebook, the most prolonged standing of the major social media platforms, is useful because of the number of friends most individuals have. You can market from your personal page, although I would caution you not to overdo it. Your friends may feel a bit used if they see constant status updates to buy your book. You can also start a business page that you can use for marketing and promoting your book(s) and services. I also warn that this option can limit your visibility because Facebook caps the number of views your business page receives. To address this issue, you can utilize their boost features and pay for advertising. Still, Facebook can be a great tool to market your book to your friends.

In addition to the traditional Facebook Status update, which can be text, pictures, and video, you now can broadcast via Facebook Live. This feature allows friends and others through adjusted viewership settings to watch you live. You could record yourself speaking about your book at a book signing or hold Q&A sessions with those watching as they post questions on the screen. You can inform the viewers on where they can connect with you, purchase your book, or be reminded of new releases. Overall, this feature makes visibility and customer engagement and interaction much more accessible. There are also similar features with Twitter (Periscope) and Instagram.

Twitter is also a great way to market your book. You have instant access to all of your followers, but you will need to be a bit more precise with your marketing communication. You are limited to a message of 280 characters or less (which is up from its original 140 characters). You will want to make sure your links to outside websites are short, so you won't run out of characters too quickly. As with Facebook, temper how much you are pushing your book on people. Too much marketing and you can lose your audience altogether.

As I stated earlier, you can also utilize Twitter's live broadcast feature, which is connected through its Periscope platform. As with Facebook Live, Periscope brings a closer connection with potential customers due to video interaction. The possibilities are massive with this form of technology.

Lastly, Instagram is proving to be the social media platform of preference. It gives you the best of both worlds–pictures and video. You can post photos of your upcoming title, shoot videos reminding people to watch for your new release, and gain some really cool followers in the process.

Videos are limited to 60 seconds, but it is enough time to share something intriguing for your followers to grab onto. If the 60 seconds is not enough, users can consider going live with Instagram's IGTV. This updated feature will allow you to stream live and recorded video for up to 10 minutes. You can also utilize the "stories" feature for both Facebook and Instagram. This feature allows you to upload 15-second clips of videos, pictures, and GIFs. There are so many options for marketing on social media. You just need to find your lane and drive.

When working with these social media platforms for your book, you will want to have banner images and profile pictures made for all three entities. These images are generally presented on your profile page. Most authors will have some sort of picture displaying their book cover and release date. I would also include an updated bio picture that features the color scheme, corresponding merchandise such as T-shirts that communicate the theme of the book, and more.

A local graphic designer can put this together for you, but I would encourage you to use **Canva**. Remember I referenced this designing tool earlier in the book? I believe this is the perfect platform to use when developing social media graphics for your book and for marketing purposes. In most cases, it's free, easy to use, and rather instant as you can download your graphics immediately after completion. It even has an app you can download on your IOS or Android device. Some of the graphics you can create include general social media graphics, Instagram, Twitter, and Facebook posts. Banner images, of which I recommend again that you have for all three social media platforms. Each graphic should be uniform in some way, to give your business a professional look that will provide credibility with potential customers. You can also produce flyers, infographics, posters, gift certificates, labels, postcards, invitations, programs, and announcement. A combination of any of these products would be beneficial in your marketing.

One of the most important things an author must do when preparing their marketing strategy is to develop consistency. This should be toward the top of the list when implementing your marketing strategy, as it is crucial to your overall marketing success. The message you send needs to be consistent, and the rate which you post must also be regular. I like to start my social media marketing efforts at least three to five months before I publish my title. This allows ample time to get the message about your upcoming book out. It also gives you plenty of time to develop new followers who will hopefully become lifetime customers.

Your marketing efforts don't stop after you publish your book either. To drive the sale of your book and gain new customers, implementing some type of social media challenge with your book(s) may be beneficial. In my first book, at the end of each chapter, I asked the reader to tweet something in response to what they read. This gets the virtual talk going about your book and also drives me to my next point on marketing, which is having a web presence through your own website and/or blog. There are many website options you can choose from. You may know of some local website designers that do great work, but perhaps you are interested in developing your own site. Here are a couple of options you can choose from:

WordPress – Known as the most massive self-hosted blogging tool, WordPress is used by many in the industry. WordPress.org may be for more experienced designers, as you can do some coding, but they also have a scaled-down version in Wordpress.com. This site allows you to use templates for blogging and/or website design. There are various features you can purchase as add-ons (domain, video, fonts, color schemes, etc.). Overall, this is one of the industry standards for web site development.

Wix – This website designing service has been in existence for some time. With it, you can design a fresh looking website that will accomplish all of your professional and personal needs. You can choose from several templates categorized from business to artist pages. They have free, monthly, and/or yearly hosting fees associated with each site. What I like about this tool is you can also obtain a business email through Google in conjunction with a purchased domain. This is a great and affordable option if you want the freedom of using cool templates without all the complicated coding found with most HTML sites.

Other website builders and blogging sites you may want to check out include Weebly, Blogger, Squarespace, and a bunch of different options that can be found online. All of these options have benefits and drawbacks, so I would encourage you to look into each genuinely to find the best fit for you.

Once you have set up your website, you can now correspond with your target market in multiple ways. Your social media accounts push customers to your web site to find more in-depth information about you as an author and your self-publishing company. You may have the ability to allow visitors to sign-up for monthly newsletters or complete query forms on your website. On most websites, the visitor can view your blog entries and contact you directly via email for additional assistance. These are just a few things I found to be critical when starting to market my book. Now that you have reached the point of marketing your book, you are ready to begin selling. In the next chapter, we will highlight where to start.

7 START SELLING

One of the most important days for a self-published author, other than hitting the publish button, is getting their first book sale. It was thrilling for me, to say the least. All of my hard work. All of the late nights. Overcoming all my doubts and fears, and I was finally able to see my first royalty payment deposited into my bank account. Now it is time for you to experience the same thing. It's time to start selling.

If you have published your book using KDP, then you are familiar with the pricing structure and calculator. KDP allows you to play around with different figures to determine what profit margin will work for you. Depending on the make of your book and the number of pages it has, KDP will specify a minimum price you cannot go below.

This leads me to my next point, which is, you can sell your book in a few different ways. The first way is to start selling your book on Amazon. This option is automatic if you have published through KDP. With this feature, you can reach a worldwide audience. Your book has the potential to touch all of North America, Europe, and Asia (for specific listings, please visit KDP for more detail). There is also the ability to have expanded distribution where your book appears on other online retailer sites, one of the largest being Barnes & Noble.

A second way for you to sell your book is through direct sales. Again, if you have published with KDP, you have the option of purchasing your own title at a discounted price (merely the production and shipping cost). As previously stated with the pricing calculator, the direct purchasing process also factors in the type of book, size, and page number. In most instances, no matter the book size, you will find a relatively inexpensive direct purchase option.

Another great way to get your book into the hands of readers is through speaking engagements. You can set up a book table for your titles and provide additional resources such as CDs, DVDs, and more. You may also consider signing your books and selling them at a higher rate at your speaking engagements or through a separate planned event. Authors find the direct sales option to be very lucrative because you are cutting out the middleman who typically distributes the product. With direct sales, you can negotiate with local retailers and book stores and do what is known as a consignment. This will get your book on more shelves. With this option, you give a portion of the sale to the business you have agreed to consign with. As a self-publishing company, you may want to consider bulk orders. There might be an organization that is excited to hear you speak or read your book. Consider developing a bulk option where you can sell large quantities of your book. Again, you have control over how much you will charge for this. Diversifying your book will also help you sell more copies. We previously mentioned publishing both print and electronic books. You can choose to publish your ebook on your own through KDP. I utilized this feature with my first book, and it made things a whole lot easier and provided an additional way to earn income.

In addition to KDP ebook publishing, there are other print-on-demand platforms where you can get your print and ebook developed. In the next chapter, we will highlight a few other print-on-demand options that can help you enlarge your reach and increase your book sales.

8 START EXPANDING

After you start selling books and conducting speaking engagements, it's time to start expanding your brand and your business. One way to do this is by publishing your book on new platforms. Below you will find some of the top competitors for self-publishing your book.

Top Print-on-Demand Options:

Lulu – Since 2002, Lulu has been considered one of the top self-publishing platforms. You can self-publish both print and electronic books when using Lulu. They also give the option of expanded distribution with Amazon, Barnes & Noble, and Ingram. You can earn royalties for your ebooks with iBooks, Amazon Kindle, Barnes & Noble, and Kobo. LuLu also specializes in calendars and photobooks. Overall, Lulu is a great way to self-publish your book. Review their web site at www.lulu.com for more information

BookBaby – Since 2011, BookBaby has helped thousands realize their publishing goals, and they've paid out millions of dollars in royalties to their authors. BookBaby offers you the largest ebook distribution network, including Amazon, Apple, Kobo, Barnes & Noble, and many other popular retailers in over 170 countries around the globe. They are the sister company to CD Baby, the world's largest online distributor of independent music. The drawback here would be the initial cost to set up your print or electronic book. Print-on-demand platforms like KDP and Lulu are free to set up, so if start-up cost is a deal-breaker, you may want to choose a different option. I encourage you to visit BookBaby's site for more details at www.bookbaby.com.

Top ebook Distributors

If you are especially interested in writing and selling ebooks, then there are several options for you. Here are a few ebook distributors to consider:

Smashwords – This company is the world's largest distributor of indie books. Smashwords distributes books to most of the major retailers, including Apple iBooks, Barnes & Noble, Sony, Kobo and the Diesel ebook store. The drawback to using this distributor is the difficulty of formatting the manuscript, so it receives approval through Smashwords and the various retailers you are interested in. Once you get the hang of proper formatting, the process may become more natural. Overall, this is a popular option for ebook authors. For more information, visit their website at www.smashwords.com.

Draft 2 Digital – This company is a digital publishing aggregator. They provide a single, easy-to-use portal where you convert your manuscript into an expertly formatted ebook. You then publish it through some of the industry's most influential retailers, including Apple iBooks, Barnes & Noble, Kobo, Scribd, Tolino, and Page Foundry. The exciting thing about this option is they will allow you to use any manuscript template and they will convert it into the proper ebook format. Additionally, they will also develop your manuscript to be used with KDP. So, in essence, they can go from an ebook to a print book. This distributor pays out monthly royalties while most others payout quarterly. The only downside is draft 2 digital is still considered the new kid on the block compared to its competitors. For more information on this distributor, visit their website at www.draft2digital.com.

You can always consider uploading and publishing your manuscript directly through the retailer. Nook, Kindle, and iBooks all have options to upload through their own sites. For Barnes & Noble, you can publish through their distributor Nook Press. They have a simple set-up wizard that walks you through the publishing process. If you decide to publish through this channel, you would be doing so with the understanding your ebook will only be available at Barnes & Noble. For more information, please visit www.nookpress.com.

KDP is the most popular among indie ebook authors as it has the most reach. Amazon KDP also has what they call Kindle Select. This feature will allow you to run promotions, such as selling your ebook at a discounted rate or even giving your ebook away for FREE! You may ask yourself, "Why would anyone give his or her ebook away for free?" This type of promotion gets your ebook into more hands and provides more traffic to your site and/or Amazon page for future sales of that specific book and other products. Most ebook distributors pay royalties between 35-70%. Amazon KDP falls into both categories. For ebooks priced between $0.99 and $2.99, the royalty is 35%. For ebooks priced $3.00-$9.99, the royalty is $70%. This is one of the highest, if not the best, royalty payment available.

I have personally used Amazon KDP, and it has been a great experience. For more information, visit kdp.amazon.com. Lastly, Apple has their own ebook publishing program called iBooks Author. This allows authors to develop very dynamic ebooks with pictures, audio, and even video. This program is not only used for ebooks, but also for digital textbooks and projects. Of all the ebook distributors, iBooks Author is pushing the envelope and is on the cutting edge of innovation. With that said, it still has its challenges. To utilize this system, you must have a Mac computer. Also, there are other fees associated with getting your ebook on the Apple iBooks store. It is important to remember if you publish with any of the direct retailers you will only be able to sell your ebook with that retailer.

As I conclude, there are many options to self-publish, both print and electronic. You don't have to box yourself in with one particular platform. I encourage you to explore your options, perhaps even have a combination of several print-on-demand and ebook services. The main point of emphasis is to get published. Don't hold back; live out your dream of becoming a self-published author. Remember, if you can find the courage to jump out of mediocrity and write, then your book is now.

ABOUT THE AUTHOR

DeMarquis Battle is the founder and president of Battle Leadership Group LLC. He is known as an up and coming servant leader within his generation. He is a visionary, entrepreneur, educator, mentor, and speaker. He holds a Bachelor of Arts degree from Siena Heights University and two Master of Arts degrees from Grace College & Seminary and Lincoln Christian University. He has also completed a postgraduate certificate in Strategic Management from Davenport University. He is married to his beautiful wife, Raynika Battle, and they have two children, Justus and Olivia-Grace.

www.ingramcontent.com/pod-product-compliance
Lightning Source LLC
Chambersburg PA
CBHW072342270726
48659CB00023B/2285